Letterland

Contents

Level 3 - Student Book 2

Let's meet Golden Girl's school friend, Gentle Ginger. Listen to how she lights up with Blue Magic sparks.

Track
72

Blue magic!

Golden Girl has a school friend called Gentle Ginger.

Golden Girl is very impressed with Gentle Ginger's gymnastic skills. She wants everyone to notice, so she asked Mr E to make Blue Magic to light her up. Blue Magic is not powerful, and it doesn't jump over letters. It just lights up Gentle Ginger so she starts to say her name when she's next to an e, i or y!

  **gé gi gy**

Letter sounds ⚑ Use your *Picture Code Cards* to compare Golden Girl and Gentle Ginger's sound. This is sometimes called a 'Soft g'.

 Listen and explore the scene with Gentle Ginger the Gymnast in the Letterland Gym.

Track 73

Gymnastics Club

Trial Package

MANAGER'S OFFICE

Gentlemen

Hygiene Hand Gel

NO GERMS

Ginger Energy Drink

DANGER

Slippery surface when wet

Orange flavour Energy Gels

Vegetable Smoothies

Gentle Ginger the Gymnast

Soft g sound

Listen again and this time look for the things in the picture that have the 'soft **g**' sound.

3

Keywords ➤

Find these items in the picture on the previous page.
Listen out for Gentle Ginger in these words.

Track
74

vegetables

orange

giraffe

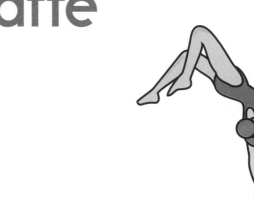

gym

gymnast

Workbook — There are specific *Workbook 2* pages for **ge**, **gi**, and **gy**.
Spend up to three lessons completing pages 2-9.

Workbook

Song

Listen to the song. If you can, join in when you listen for the second time.

Track 75

Listen to the song!

I am Gentle Ginger.
I love somersaulting,
cartwheeling, vaulting
and swinging on a bar.

This is Gentle Ginger.
She loves somersaulting,
cartwheeling, vaulting
and swinging on a bar.

Look for Gentle Ginger
in the Blue Magic Light.
She works with all her might.
What a gymnastic star!

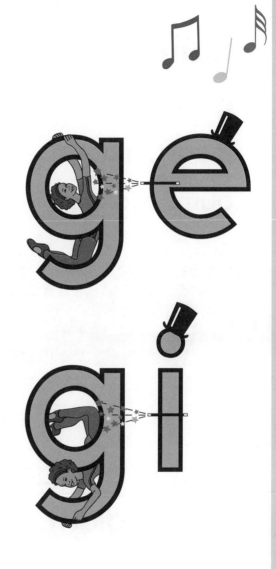

Search and read Do not try to read the whole song, but can you read the words that have Gentle Ginger in them?

5

Build some **ge**, **gi** and **gy** words using *Phonics Online, Letter Sound Cards* or the *Picture Code Cards*.

Code Card

Build it!

gem, germ

magic, margin

gym, allergy.

Let's read!

Use the Sound Slide trick to blend the sounds together and read the words. Then try reading the sentences with more fluency.

That is a huge, gentle giant.

The gem stones look magical.

Pair work   Work in pairs. Read the sentences to a partner as fluently as you can.

Often there's a silent **d** before words with a soft **g** sound.

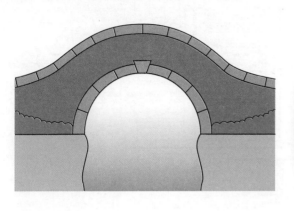

bridge

fridge   edge   hedge

Read it!

A silent duck is on the bridge.

A silent duck is by the fridge.

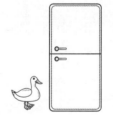

A silent duck is on the edge.

A silent duck is behind the hedge.

Pair work   Read the sentences to a partner as fluently as you can.
Then complete the exercises on pages 10-11 of *Workbook 2.*

Workbook

Story time

Vegetables!

1. Look at the pictures and discuss what the story might be about.
2. Read the story together.
3. Search for all the '**ge**', '**gi**' and '**gy**'words.
4. See how much you can read!

It's winter in Letterland. Vicky Violet is delivering vegetables.

It is so cold that the engine in her van has stopped working.

"How will I manage without my van?" says Vicky.
"I'll help you," says Walter.

 Reading

Fluency - Reading fluently is a skill which can be achieved through familiarity with the text. Listen, then read the story.

"Look! A wheelbarrow works in the snow and ice. We will just need lots of energy to push it!"

They fill the wheelbarrow with lots of winter vegetables, like carrots and cabbages.

They push the vegetables to the King's castle. "That's so generous! I was just about to make a cake with carrots and ginger. Come in and join me!" says Kicking King.

Now try writing

When you have finished this page, do the related **Vegetables!** exercise on page 12 of *Workbook 2*.

Workbook

Stickers > Complete the sticker activity in *Workbook 2*, page 13.

Listen > Complete the exercises in *Workbook 2*, pages 14-15.

Talk time > Past tense. Read the story and use a dictionary to look up any words you don't know. Discuss the meanings.

An Ice Age

Once upon a time, many years ago, it was very cold. There was lots of ice and glaciers.

It was called an Ice Age.

Giant animals like saber-toothed tigers and woolly mammoths lived on our planet.

Ice Age people lived 35,000 year ago. They hunted animals and lived in caves.

Pair work Work in pairs. Read these facts about the last Ice Age to a partner as fluently as you can. Remember to use a dictionary for words you don't understand.

Kicking King stays silent!

Kicking King loves kicking but Noisy Nick has a knack of getting in his way. Instead of kicking and making his sound he frowns and stays silent.

Letter sounds Use your *Picture Code Cards* to review Kicking King and Noisy Nick's sounds. Then look how Kicking King stays silent when they are together.

Code Card 11

 **Explore**

Listen to the story about what happens when Kicking King and Noisy Nick come together in a word.

Track 81

Kicking King stays quiet in front of Noisy Nick

kn digraph

Listen again and this time look for the things in the picture that have the 'kn' sound.

Find these items in the picture. Listen for the '**kn**' sound at the start of the words.

knit

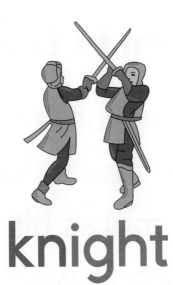

knight

knot

knock

knife

Workbook — When you have finished this page, do the Keywords exercises on pages 16-17, *Workbook 2*.

13

Song → Listen to the song. If you can, join in when you listen for the second time.

Track 83

Listen to the song!

If you want to know
who upsets the King
and makes his frown so black,
someone who's a nuisance,
guess who has the knack?

If you want to know
who upsets the King
or why he might not kick,
you know who
you should talk to.
Just ask Noisy Nick!

Search and read

Do not try to read the whole song, but can you read the words that have Kicking King and Noisy Nick next to each other?

Word Building

Build some **kn** words using the *Picture Code Cards, Letter Sound Cards* or *Phonics Online.*

Code Card

Build it!

knew, know, knot, knight.

Let's read!

Use the Sound Slide trick to blend the sounds together and read the words. Then try reading the sentences with more fluency.

The knights fight at night.

I know how to tie knots.

Don't knock the knife!

Read with fluency

Read these sentences to two friends, working on improving your reading fluency each time. Then complete pages 18-19, *Workbook 2.*

Workbook

Story ➤ Listen to why you will occasionally hear Clever Cat making her usual sound next to Harry Hat Man as his hat has blown off!

Clever Cat doesn't sneeze!

 Clever Cat says 'c' in words and Harry Hat Man says 'h'.

 When they sit together his hairy hat tickles her nose and she sneezes 'ch!'

Occasionally though, Harry's hat blows off in the wind.

Clever Cat doesn't sneeze. She says 'c' again and Harry is too startled to speak!

Explore ➤ Listen to the story about the wind blowing away Harry Hat Man's hat. Clever Cat's nose does not tickle, so she does not sneeze!

Track 85

Clever Cat and Harry Hat Man

Listen again Listen again and this time look for the things in the picture that have **ch** making a 'c' sound.

17

Find these items in the picture. Listen for Clever Cat's 'c' sound and a silent 'h' in each word.

Track 86

school

choir

mechanic

chemical

orchestra

Workbook

When you have finished this page, do the Keywords exercises on pages 20-21, *Workbook 2*.

Workbook

Song

Listen to the song. If you can, join in when you listen for the second time.

Track
87

Listen to the song!

It's windy in Letterland – the gusts come and go.

When they come look out for them –

it can really blow!

School is a gusty place, of that I have no doubt.

Harry is left speechless,

but Clever Cat cries out!   (x2)

Harry's hat blows off in orchestra.

In choir he makes no noise.

It's gusty too at Christmas time,

so he just plays with toys!

Search and read

Do not try to read the whole song, but can you read the words that have Clever Cat and Harry Hat Man in them?

19

Build some **ch** words using the *Picture Code Cards* or *Letter Sound Cards*.

Code Card

Build it!

school,
mechanic,
archive.

Let's read!

Use the Sound Slide trick to blend the sounds together and read the words. Then try reading the sentences with more fluency.

He has a stomach ache.

She is part of the school orchestra.

Read with fluency

Read these sentences to two friends, working on improving your reading fluency each time. Then complete pages 22-23, *Workbook 2*.

Workbook

Story

Mr Mean-E makes spelling tricky by making e's sound like Mr A.

Track 88

Mr Mean-E

Mr Mean-E is an old man who likes to make spelling difficult. He tries to trick us by looking like an e but sounding like an a.

He is too mean to be seen very often in words, but you can see him in the word 'they'.

 Letter sounds

Use your *Picture Code Cards* to show Mr Mean-E. He is green to remind you he sounds like Mr A.

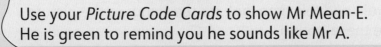 Code Card

21

Listen to the story about Mr Mean-E making spelling tricky by making a sound like Mr A.

Mr Mean-E

Listen again

Listen again and this time look for the things in the picture that have the 'e' sound.

Find these items in the picture. Listen for Mr Mean-E's sound in each word.

grey

prey

8
eight

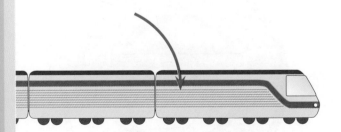

freight

sleigh

Workbook When you have finished this page, do the Keywords exercises on pages 24-25, *Workbook 2.*

Song → Listen to the song. If you can, join in when you listen for the second time.

Track 91

Listen to the song!

Hee, hee, hee,
I'm Mr Mean-E.
I say 'a'
in the word they.

I'll be glad so long
as you spell they wrong!

Hee, hee, hee,
I'm Mr Mean-E.
I say 'a'
in the word grey.

I'll be glad so long
as you spell grey wrong!

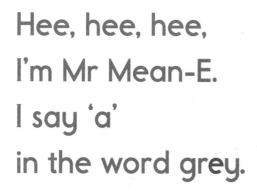

24

NOTE: Spelling *Grey* and *gray* are two different spellings of the same word. *Gray* is used more in the U.S., while *grey* is more common in other English-speaking countries.

Build some **e** words using the *Picture Code Cards*.
The **y** is a silent look-out man. Use a plain letter shape.

Code Card

Build it!

hey, they, grey,
obey, prey.

Let's read! ▶

Use the Sound Slide trick to blend the sounds together and read
the words. Then try reading the sentences with more fluency.

The osprey has the prey.

The sky is dark and grey.

The reindeer pulls the sleigh.

Read with fluency

Read these sentences to two friends, working on improving your reading
fluency each time. Then complete pages 26-27, *Workbook 2*.

Workbook

Story time

Time for School

1. Look at the pictures and discuss what the story might be about.
2. Read the story together.
3. Search for all the '**kn**', '**ch**' and '**e**' words.
4. See how much you can read!

Fix-it Max gets up at six o'clock. He likes to exercise in the morning before school.

Mr Mean-E gets up at eight o'clock. It's a grey day.

Noisy Nick gets up at nine o'clock and reads the newspaper on his knee. No school, Nick?

 Reading

Fluency - Reading fluently is a skill which can be achieved through familiarity with the text. Listen, then read the story.

Talking Tess gets up at ten o'clock and brushes her teeth. She knows she doesn't want to get toothache!

But do you know who likes to snooze all day? Zig Zag Zebra. Knock on the door and say, 'GET OUT OF BED!'

What time do you think they go to bed at night? Do you know what time you go to bed when you have school in the morning?

Now try writing

When you have finished this page, do the related **Time for School** exercise on pages 28-29 of *Workbook 2*.

Workbook

Stickers  Complete the sticker activity in *Workbook 2*, page 30.

Listen Complete the exercises in *Workbook 2*, pages 32-33.

Talk time Listen to the conversation.
Then you try asking a partner about their health.

Aches and Pains!

Questions	Answers
Do you have any aches or pains?	No, I am very well thank you. Yes, I have a (tooth, stomach, head) ache. Yes, my (hand, leg, foot) hurts/aches.
How long have you had it?	It's been aching for (2 hours) now.
Have you been to the doctor/ the hospital?	Yes, I went to the doctor yesterday. No, I haven't been to the doctor.
Have you taken any medecine?	Yes, I took a (headache tablet). No, I haven't taken any medicine.

My arm aches!

What's the matter?

Pair work Pretend you have an illness or you have hurt yourself.
Describe what is wrong to your partner. Swap roles and repeat.

Story  Mr 'Tion has a little trick to help you spell lots of words.

Track
96

Mr 'Tion

In Letterland there is a teacher called Mr 'Tion. He had a tea party for his class, but first they had to do a spelling quiz.

He asked, 'Can anyone spell my name?' Many children tried spelling it with 'sh' but Noisy Nick spelt it correctly. Mr 'Tion said 'Here's the Tea I Owe Nick. Remembering that will help you spell it correctly, too!'

Letter Sounds Use your *Picture Code Cards* to show Mr 'Tion.

Code Card

29

Listen to the story about Noisy Nick's teacher talking about the 'Tea I Owe Nick'!

Track 97

Mr 'Tion

2 letters: 1 sound

Listen again and this time look for the things in the picture that have the 'tion' sound.

Find these items in the picture. Listen for the **'tion'** sound in these words.

caution

portion

dictionary

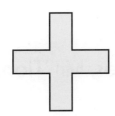

addition   subtraction

Workbook When you have finished this page, do the Keywords exercises on pages 34-35, *Workbook 2*.

31

Listen to the song!

Mr 'Tion:
Hello, hello, please pay attention.
I'm your teacher.
Time for action. I am Mr 'Tion.
Right now it's time to do addition.
After that we'll do subtraction.

Chorus: Yes, Mr 'Tion.

Mr 'Tion:
And then we'll do multiplication.
After that we'll study fractions.

Chorus: Yes, Mr 'Tion

Mr 'Tion:
Next we'll study new inventions, transportation, navigation, aviation, famous men in exploration.

Chorus: Yes, Mr 'Tion

Mr 'Tion:
Then we'll study punctuation, dictionary information, the Industrial Revolution, and some points on evolution.

Chorus: Yes, Mr 'Tion

Mr 'Tion: Then, if, my dears, you've paid attention, on completion of a dictation, there'll be time for recreation.

Chorus: Yes, Mr 'Tion!

Tricky! Many of the words that have **'tion'** at the end are quite long. Let your teacher explain some of the meanings.

Word Building

Build some **tion** words using the *Picture Code Cards* or *Phonics Online*.

Code Card

Build it!

caution, portion, fraction, invention.

Let's read!

Use the Sound Slide trick to blend the sounds together and read the words. Then try reading the sentences with more fluency.

I like addition!

$2 + 2 = 4$ ✔

I do not like fractions.

$\frac{1}{2} + \frac{1}{2} = 2$ ✗

I must make corrections.

$\frac{1}{2} + \frac{1}{2} = 1$ ✔

Read with fluency

Read these sentences to two friends, working on improving your reading fluency each time. Then complete pages 36-37, *Workbook 2*.

Workbook

Track 100

Talking Tess sneezes!

As Urgent Ur runs past Talking Tess, he hears her sneeze, just like Clever Cat does sometimes 'ch'. Urgent Ur always overpowers the Magic **e** at the end to make sure it can't turn his stolen umbrella into a Vowel Man.

Odd Endings

Over 40 useful words end in ture. Many are mis-spelt c-h-e-r. Unless the word is 'teacher' it's generally best to spell it ture.

Code Card

Explore ⟶ Listen to the story about Tess sneezing when she is out in nature.

Track 101

Tess sneezes as Urgent Ur breaks Magic e's wand.

Listen again Listen again and this time look for the things in the picture that have the '**ture**' sound.

35

Find these items in the picture on the previous page.
Listen for the '**ture**' sound at the end of the words.

Track 102

picture

vulture

sculpture

furniture

puncture

Workbook

When you have finished this page, do the Keywords exercises on pages 38-39, *Workbook 2*.

Workbook

Song ➤ Listen to the song. If you can, join in when you listen for the second time.

Track 103

Listen to the song!

Sneezing! Sneezing! Have you heard
Talking Tess sneezing?

Is she allergic? I don't know.
But she sneezes when she's out in nature.
She sneezes in pastures, when she's on adventures.
And she sneezes near creatures like vultures.

Sneezing! Sneezing! Urgent Ur passes Tess sneezing!

Is she allergic? He doesn't know.
But she sneezes when she looks at sculpture.
She sneezes on her bike, when she has a puncture.
And even when she's sitting on furniture!

Sneezing! Sneezing! Have you heard
Talking Tess sneezing? Sneezing! Have you heard
Talking Tess sneezing?
"Ture!"

Search and read Do not try to read the whole song, but can you read the words that have Talking Tess sneezing in them?

37

Word Building ▶

Build some **ture** words using the *Picture Code Cards* or *Letter Sound Cards*.

Code Card

Build it!

capture, picture, puncture, vulture.

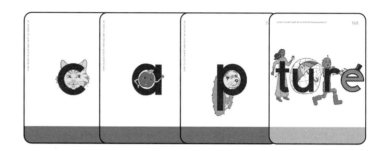

Let's read! ▶

Use the Sound Slide trick to blend the sounds together and read the words. Then try reading the sentences with more fluency.

The bike has a puncture.

It's a sculpture of a vulture.

Read with fluency

Read these sentences to two friends, working on improving your reading fluency each time. Then complete pages 40-41, *Workbook 2*.

Workbook

Story Giant All steals and eats apples in Letterland so when you see his long legs, don't expect the usual 'a' sound.

Track 104

Giant All!

Giant All is so tall that **all** you can see of him in words are his two long legs!

Giant All loves apples. He often strides into words and steals apples. If you spot his longs legs in a word, don't expect to hear the usual 'a' sound. You'll just hear Giant All, calling his own name 'all'!

Letter sounds Use your *Picture Code Cards* to show the tallest man of all, Giant All.

Code Card

39

Listen to the story about Giant All stealing apples in Letterland.

Ball stall

3 for 2
small balls

Giant All

 Listen again

Listen again and this time look for the things in the picture that have the 'all' sound.

Find these items in the picture. Listen for the '**all**' sound at the end of the words.

ball

fall

wall

holdall

stall

Workbook

When you have finished this page, do the Keywords exercises on pages 42-43, *Workbook 2*.

Listen to the song. If you can, join in when you listen for the second time.

Track 107

Listen to the song!

Giant All is so tall,

that he makes me feel small.

Giant All is so tall

he can reach almost all

of the apples on hand,

here in Letterland.

But if Giant All were to fall

with a THUD off the wall,

then he might not be

quite so tall after all!

Search and read

Do not try to read the whole song, but can you read the words that have Giant All in them?

Giant All is very lazy. He often leans back on a word to eat an apple. When he leans on a word you only see one of his legs. But don't let that fool you. It's still Giant All. He likes leaning on the words most, so, ways, ready and though most of all.

Word Building Use your *Picture Code Cards* to show Giant All leaning on words. Build some prefix **al-** words.

Build it!

almost, also, always.

Workbook When you have finished this page, do the exercises on pages 44-45, *Workbook 2*.

43

Giant All

also

already   always

altogether

although   almost

Spelling helpers! Knowing this story helps prevent common spelling errors such as 'allmost', and 'allso'.

Story ▶ Let's meet another giant in Letterland and see what happens when he pulls up other words to lean on.

Track 109

Giant Full is a lazy old giant. He tries to help Mr U collect umbrellas. He pushes and pulls them into u's until they are full.

But he's very lazy, so he often pulls up a word next to him to lean on. When he leans on a word, be careful, as you will only see one of his legs!

Spelling helpers Knowing this story helps prevent common spelling errors such as 'carefull', and 'helpfull'.

Code Card

45

Explore

Listen to the story about Giant Full leaning on lots of words at the Letterland market.

Track 110

Giant Full resting on words

 Listen again

Listen again and this time look for the things in the picture that have the '**ful**' sound.

Listen and repeat the words. Can you think of any more words where you can hear Giant Full resting?

mouthful

armful

handful

spoonful

playful

Workbook

When you have finished this page, do the Keywords exercises on pages 46-47, *Workbook 2*.

Song ➤ Listen to the song. If you can, join in when you listen for the second time.

Track 112

Listen to the song!

Giant Full, Giant Full!
Please don't push us.
Please don't pull us.
No, no, no.

We are hopeful you'll be careful.
Don't be frightful, don't be painful.
Please don't grab us by the armful,
just a handful, please, please, please.

We are hopeful you'll be lawful,
tactful, thoughtful,
and not awful.
We'll be thankful if you're
skilful, helpful, useful, yes,
yes, please.

Search and read · Do not try to read the whole song.
Can you read the words that have Giant Full in them?

Build some **ful** words using the *Letter Sound Cards, Picture Code Cards* or *Phonics Online*.

Code Card

Build it!

useful, restful, handful, playful.

Let's read!

Use the Sound Slide trick to blend the sounds together and read the words. Then try reading the sentences with more fluency.

The farmer has a handful of seeds.

He takes a nice big mouthful.

Read with fluency

Read these sentences to two friends, working on improving your reading fluency each time. Then complete pages 48-49, *Workbook*

Workbook

49

Wonderful Creations

1. Look at the pictures and discuss what the story might be about.
2. Read the story together.
3. Search for all the '**tion**', '**ture**', '**al-**' and '**-ful**' words.
4. See how much you can read!

Bouncy Ben has red, yellow, blue and green blocks. He likes construction.

"Can we make a tower?" asks Talking Tess.

"I am skilful with blocks. Can I join in?" asks Jumping Jim.

 Reading

Fluency - Reading fluently is a skill which can be achieved through familiarity with the text. Listen, then read the story.

 Track 113

"Can I add a handful to make the creation higher?" asks Harry Hat Man.

"Look out, Ben!" says Lucy Lamp Light, loudly. But it is already too late. The construction collapses.

"That always happens! We can all help to make a new tower and take a picture," says Talking Tess. Harry Hat Man says he will help to make it higher and more wonderful.

Now try writing

When you have finished this page, do the related **Wonderful Creations** exercise on pages 50-51 of *Workbook 2.*

Workbook

Stickers ➜ Complete the sticker activity in *Workbook 2*, page 52.

Listen ➜ Complete the exercises in *Workbook 2*, pages 54-55.

Talk time ➜ Listen to the ways of describing what you would like to do in the future. Talk about your hopes and dreams!

Track 116

In the Future

Questions	Possible Answers
What job would you like to do, in the future?	I would like to be a/an ... (baker/teacher) I hope I can be a/an ... (explorer/astronaut) It would be nice to be a/an ... (climber/dentist)
Where would you like to live, in the future?	I'd like to live in a ... (tree house/city/town) I hope to live ... (with my family/on my own)
Would you like to get married, in the future?	Yes, it would be nice to get married. No, I'd prefer not to get married.
Would you like to have children, in the future?	Yes, I would like to have .... children. I might want to have children. I'm not sure. No, I don't think I want to have children.
What goals do you have for the future?	One day, I hope to ... (climb Everest/go into space/live on a farm/ live in a big house/be rich/be famous/travel the world/make lots of people happy/plant lots of trees)

?

Remember your goals are *yours*!
Look up words in a dictionary to decribe
your goals in life.

52

Pair work

Work with a partner talking about what they would like to do in the future. Ask questions. Swap roles and repeat.

Candle Magic!

When a Magic e is next to Lucy Lamp Light sometimes the magic sparks change Lucy into a large magical candle. When the candle is burning it can send magic sparks up and over one letter.

Letter sounds
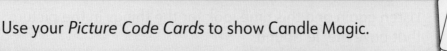
Use your *Picture Code Cards* to show Candle Magic.

Code Card

53

Listen to the story about what happens when Lucy turns into a large Magic Candle. Can friends come together to the rescue?

Candle Magic

Listen again

Listen again and this time look for the things in the picture that have the '**le**' sound.

Find these items in the picture. Listen for the '**le**' sound at the end of the words.

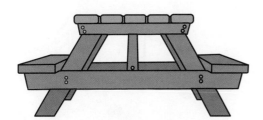

table

stable

apple

bottle

puzzle

Workbook — When you have finished this page, do the Keywords exercises on pages 56-57, *Workbook 2*.

Song ➤ Listen to the song. If you can, join in when you listen for the second time.

Track 120

Listen to the song!

Suddenly the lady can

become a magic candle.

The Magic E beside her

is the magic candle's handle.

Put it in the middle

of a tiny little table.

Then just shoot the magic sparks

as quick as you are able.

Search and read Do not try to read the whole song, but can you read the words that have Candle Magic in them?

Build some **le** words using the *Letter Sound Cards* or *Picture Code Cards*.

Build it!

able, cable, maple, table, stable, bible.

Let's read!

Use the Sound Slide trick to blend the sounds together and read the words. Then try reading the sentences with more fluency.

That tree is a maple.

The apple is on the table.

The candle is little.

You know some Letterlanders have Best Friends.
Now see how they come to the rescue by blocking magic.

Best Friends to the Rescue

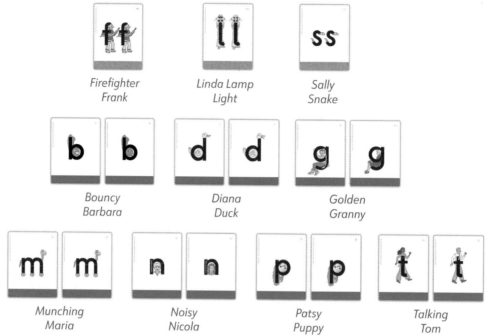

Firefighter
Frank

Linda Lamp
Light

Sally
Snake

Bouncy
Barbara

Diana
Duck

Golden
Granny

Munching
Maria

Noisy
Nicola

Patsy
Puppy

Talking
Tom

Magic Endings work so well in Letterland that the Vowel Men get tired having to appear in so many words. We can't undo magic so what happens? Best Friends come to the rescue!

Best friends

Talk about 'best friends'. Who is your best friend? Why are they your best friend? How does your best friend help you?

Act out the story of Best Friends protecting a short vowel from magic.

Code Card

idle

meaning: inactive, not working

middle

Use some **Best Friends** and build words using the *Letter Sound Cards* or *Picture Code Cards*.

Code Card

Build it!

apple, battle

little, middle

kettle, peddle

wobble, bottle

puddle, shuffle.

Note: If there are two consonants, no best friend is needed. For example: ca<u>nd</u>le, fre<u>ck</u>le, ti<u>ck</u>le, ju<u>ng</u>le, si<u>mp</u>le, te<u>mp</u>le.

Story ▶ Listen to the story about what happens when Mr e puts his hat down to make this exciting Magic Ending.

Track 122

Do you remember?

When Noisy Nick and Golden Girl sit together, they are so happy, they sing!

Magic Ending -ing

Magic -ing was made by accident! Just after Mr E invented his Magic e's he took his hat off and rested it on an -ing ending. His hat was still full of magic because the -ing ending became magical, too. Mr E decided it was quite exciting to have -ing as a magic ending.

Letter Sounds Use your *Picture Code Cards* to show Magic -ing ending. **Code Card**

Listen and explore the picture for all the words with this exciting Magic Ending.

Track 123

Magic Ending -ing

🚩 **Listen again**

Listen again and this time look for the things in the picture that have an 'ing' ending.

Keywords ➡

Find these items in the picture on the previous page.
Listen for the **'ing'** sound at the end of the words.

Track 124

driving

racing

skating

riding

smoking

Workbook

When you have finished this page, do the Keywords
exercises on pages 60-61, Workbook 2.

Workbook

Song ➤ Listen to the song. If you can, join in when you listen for the second time.

Track 125

Listen to the song!

Annie Apple:
Keep your eyes peeled
in the Reading Direction.
Single vowels like me
often need protection!

Ing:
We are a Magic Ending.
Today we have come here
to shoot our sparks right on to you,
and make you disappear!

Annie Apple:
Help! Help!
I'm going to disappear!
Come quickly to the rescue!

Peter Puppy (with Patsy Puppy):
Friend to the rescue!
My friend's here!
Never fear!
We won't let you disappear!

Ing:
What a shame! What a shame!
We wanted to play
the Naming Game,
but Annie Apple made such a
fuss that now her two friends
are stopping us!

All:
So let's all clap instead, shall we?

Clapping, clapping, clapping.
We're just as happy clapping. x2

Tapping, tapping, tapping.
We're just as happy tapping. x2

Search and read — Do not try to read the whole song, but can you read the words that have Magic **ing** in them?

63

Build some **ing** words using the *Picture Code Cards*.
Show how adding a Best Friend can block the magic!

Code Card

Build it! Best Friends to the Rescue

hoping - hopping

Let's read! ➤

Use the Sound Slide trick to blend the sounds together and read the words. Then try reading the sentences with more fluency.

Riding a bike is exciting.

The mouse is escaping.

That volcano is exploding!

Read with fluency — Read these sentences to two friends, working on improving your reading fluency each time. Then complete pages 58-59, *Workbook 2*

Workbook

Story ▶ Just like Magic e, there's another Magic Ending -ed that makes three different sounds.

Track 126

Magic Ending ed

When Mr E invented Magic e's, Eddy Elephant was envious.

"Can I do that trick as well?" he asked.

"That's a good idea," decided Mr E.

"Wear my hat and take my wand. You'll need a friend on the end, too."

Eddy Elephant chose Dippy Duck. That's why you'll often see these two together in a new Magic Ending.

Listen to the story about Eddy Elephant and Dippy Duck coming together in this Magic Ending.

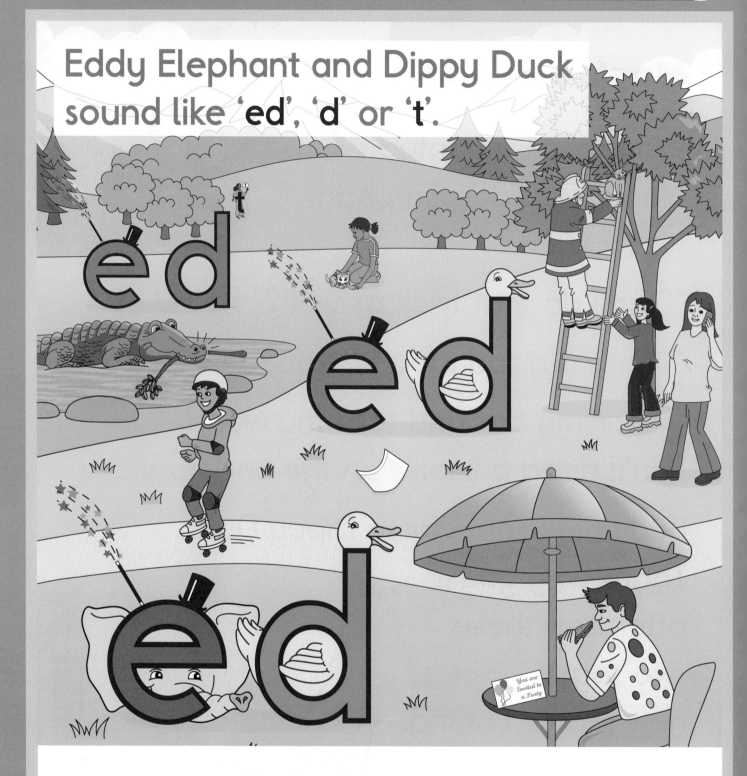

Eddy Elephant and Dippy Duck sound like 'ed', 'd' or 't'.

Magic Ending -ed

Listen again

Listen again and this time look for the things in the picture that have an 'ed' ending.

Eddy Elephant and Dippy Duck

In this ending both Eddy Elephant and Dippy Duck are saying 'ĕ' and 'd' as **expected**.

Best Friends to the Rescue

batted, dotted, nodded, spotted.

Think about these Keywords with the -**ed** ending making the 'ed' sound. Can you think of any more?

Track 129

faded

You are Invited to a Party

invited

skated

voted

spotted

Workbook

When you have finished this page, do the Keywords exercises on pages 64-65, Workbook 2.

Workbook

Eddy Elephant plays the Disappearing Game

Sometimes, Eddy Elephant plays the Disappearing Game. Listen, his sound has **disappear⌒ed.**

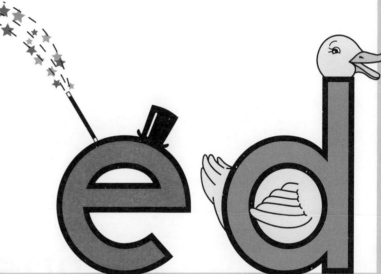

Best Friends to the Rescue

hugged, hummed rubbed, grabbed.

Blocking Magic

Use your *Picture Code Cards* to show how Best Friends come to the Rescue and block magic sparks.

Code Card

Think about these Keywords with the -**ed** ending making the 'd' sound. Can you think of any more?

smiled

phoned

lined

surprised

saved

Workbook

When you have finished this page, do the Keywords exercises on pages 66-67, *Workbook 2*.

Workbook

This is the third of three sounds of the Magic Ending -**ed**.

Track 132

Eddy Elephant and Dippy Duck play the Disappearing Game

Sometimes both Eddy Elephant and Dippy Duck play the Disappearing Game! They have both vanished, with only Talking Tess spotting them go!

vanished^t

Best Friends to the Rescue

hoped - hopped, slipped, dripped, dropped.

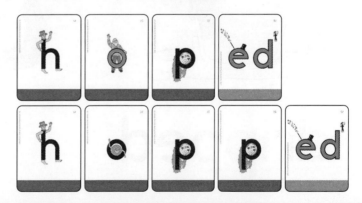

Think about these Keywords with the -**ed** ending making the 't' sound. Can you think of any more?

Track 133

baked

stroked

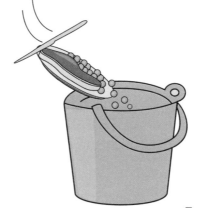

scraped

dripped

snapped

Workbook

When you have finished this page, do the Keywords exercises on pages 68-69, *Workbook 2*.

Workbook

Build some **-ed** words using the *Letter Sound Cards* or *Picture Code Cards*.

Code Card

Build it!

skated

smiled

hoped

Let's read!

Use the Sound Slide trick to blend the sounds together and read the words. Then try reading the sentences with more fluency.

She skated so well.

She phoned her sister.

He jumped over the hurdle.

Read with fluency

Read these sentences to two friends, working on improving your reading fluency each time. Then complete pages 70-71, *Workbook 2.*

Workbook

Counting!

1. Look at the pictures and discuss what the story might be about.
2. Read the story together.
3. Search for all the '**le**', '**ing**' and '**ed**' words.
4. See how much you can read!

"I like counting. I'll count everything today!" says Noisy Nick.

The sun was shining as he counted the beads on his mum's necklace.

He smiled as he counted the notes on the notice board. Are you able to count them?

  Reading If you struggle with the meaning of a word, remember you can use a dictionary to look it up!

 Track 134

He looked happy as he counted the nuts on the table. Are you able to count them?

He never stops counting things. Next, he grinned as he counted the newspapers in the shop.

Is there anything you can't count Noisy Nick?
"Well I can't count all the needles on those pine trees," he says.
(The thin leaves on pine trees are called needles!)

Now try writing

When you have finished this page, do the related **Counting on the Farm** exercise on pages 72-73 of *Workbook 2*.

Workbook

Stickers Complete the sticker activity in *Workbook 2*, pages 74.

Listen Complete the exercises in *Workbook 2*, pages 76-77.

Talk time This talk time is all about expressing preference. Listen to the people talking about celebrations, then you try.

Track 137

Celebrations!

Questions	
Would you rather...	go to a big party with fireworks, or a small party with friends?
Would you rather...	go to a loud party with lots of music and dancing, or a quiet dinner party?
Would you prefer to...	go to a fancy dress party in a costume, or wear your nicest clothes?
Would you prefer to...	be a child at a celebration, or an adult?
Answers	Explain your answers.
I'd rather... I'd prefer to...	
Vocabulary	musicians, a band, dancers, fireworks, costumes, party food, cakes, ceremonies

Pair work Work with a partner to talk about your celebration preferences. Swap roles and repeat.

Review Robots capturing Vowel Men.

Work in pairs

1. Point and say the sound.
2. Say two words for each spelling pattern.
3. Read the short passage below.

Read-along!

Track **138**

At night I think I can hear fairies in the air near my ear.

Phonics Readers

Two stories in *Phonics Readers - Blue Series, Book 10*, feature the phonic elements in this Unit.

Bears at the fair

A fairy story

Review Clever Cat as a hissing snake.

  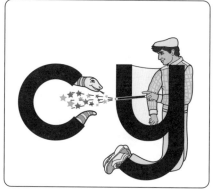

1. Point and say the sound.
2. Say two words for each spelling pattern.
3. Read the short passage below.

Track 139

Read-along!

Lucy rides her bicycle into the city. It is a cold day. The road is icy. Lucy's face feels like ice. Her nose turns red. "I look like a clown! I could join the circus!" she says.

Review Gentle Ginger the Gymnast!

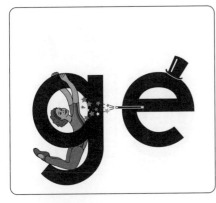  

Work in pairs

1. Point and say the sound.
2. Say two words for each spelling pattern.
3. Read the short passage below.

Read-along!

Track
140

A gymnast went to the gym to do gymnastics, but she had no energy. She ate an orange. That filled her with energy.
"An orange is like magic!"
she said.

Review Tricky spellings!

1. Point and say the sound.
2. Say two words for each spelling pattern.
3. Read the short passage below.

Track 141

Read-along!

This man with grey hair
is eighty-eight years old.
He likes to sing in a choir.
Sometimes his knees ache
when he stands and sings
in the choir for a long time!

Review A prefix, a suffix and odd endings!

Work in Pairs

1. Point and say the sound.
2. Say two words for each spelling pattern.
3. Read the short passage below.

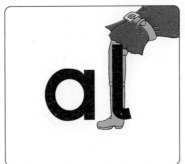

Track 142

Read-along!

The wonderful creatures in our seas are dying. We need action to save our seas from pollution. We must always be careful to protect the future of all creatures.

Review Magic Endings

1. Point and say the sound.
2. Say two words for each spelling pattern.
3. Read the short passage below.

Read-along!

Tim had been riding his horse for a while.
He needed a rest. He jumped down, stroked
his horse and divided an apple between them.
Tim smiled - the horse was not able!

Now you know all of the spelling patterns for Level 3. Use your *Picture Code Cards* to revise them.

Code Card

Revise all the sounds and spelling patterns from Level 3 using *Phonics Online* or the *Picture Code Cards*.

Quick Dash

1. Can you say the sound?
2. Can you think of a word with this sound?

/air/ /ear/ /air/

Just make the sound /s/.

Just make the sound /j/.

/n/ /k/ /ay/

/shun/ /cher/ /orl/ /orl/ /ful/

/ul/ /ing/ /ed/ /d/ /t/

Workbook

When you have completed a Quick Dash, there is a short test in *Workbook 2*, pages 78-79.

Workbook

83

Congratulations!

You've finished Fix-it Phonics Level 3!
There's a certificate for you in
your Workbook.

Letterland

Certificate!

This is to certify that

....

has finished

LETTERLAND® Fix-it Phonics Level 3

....
Your Letterland Teacher

....
Date

www.letterland.com